Book of 1 Peter Bible Studies

Books by Paul J. Bucknell

Allowing the Bible to speak to our lives today!

- Overcoming Anxiety: Finding Peace, Discovering God
- Reaching Beyond Mediocrity: Being an Overcomer
- The Life Core: Discovering the Heart of Great Training
- The Godly Man: When God Touches a Man's Life
- Redemption Through the Scriptures/ Study Guide
- Godly Beginnings for the Family
- Principles and Practices of Biblical Parenting
- Building a Great Marriage
- The Lord Your Healer: Discover Him and Find...
- Christian Premarital Counseling Manual for Counselors
- Relational Discipleship: Cross Training
- Running the Race: Overcoming Lusts
- The Bible Teaching Commentary on Genesis
- The Bible Teaching Commentary on Romans
- Book of Romans Bible Study Questions
- Book of Ephesians Bible Studies
- Walking with Jesus: Abiding in Christ
- Inductive Bible Studies in Titus
- Life Transformation: A Monthly ... on Romans 12:9-21
- Book of 1 Peter Bible Studies: Living in a Fallen World
- Satan's Four Stations: The Destroyer is Destroyed
- 3 X E Discipleship (Discipler and Disciple)
- Life in the Spirit!
- Take Your Next Step into Ministry
- Training Leaders for Ministry
- Study Guide for Jonah: Understanding God's Heart

Check out our digital libraries at
www.foundationsforfreedom.net

Book of 1 Peter Bible Studies

Living Hope in a Fallen World

—Basic and Advanced Questions—

Paul J. Bucknell

Book of 1 Peter Bible Studies: Living Hope in a Fallen World

Copyright ©2018 Paul J. Bucknell

Paperback:

ISBN-13: 978-1-61993-104-6

Also as eBook:

ISBN-13: 978-1-61993-103-9

www.bffbible.org

www.foundationsforfreedom.net

3276 Bainton St., Pittsburgh, PA 15212, USA

The NASB version is used unless otherwise stated.
New American Standard Bible ©1960, 1995 used by permission, Lockman Foundation www.lockman.org.

All rights reserved. Limited production is acceptable without prior permission for home and educational use. For extensive reproduction or questions please contact Paul Bucknell at info@foundationsforfreedom.net.

Usage of Study Questions

These guidelines will help you make the most of these basic and advanced study questions for your personal study as well as teach you how to use them as a Bible study leader.

General Overview

This book includes an introductory commentary on 1 Peter that discuses the background of the book and includes an outline, map, overview of 1 Peter word studies, and introductory descriptions of Peter, the author, and the scattered flock that Peter wrote to.

Each section of 1 Peter is broken up into teaching or study sections. There is a set of basic and advanced questions for each section. We use the NASB translation because it tends toward being a more literal translation, though we encourage your use of other translations to enrich your study. Both basic and advanced questions are meant to lead you into the discovery and application of the scripture passage.

Basic Questions

Basic study questions can be categorized in three ways:

Biblical Questions
The answers to Biblical questions will be found right in the Bible passage. These questions will encourage one to ask, "What does the passage actually say?" These questions always include the verse number in the question itself or at the end of the question in parentheses, like "(3)." If you use a different version, keep the NASB handy in case your text doesn't quite match the question. We've left some space after each question to help you foster the discipline of writing down your answers.

Thought Questions
The answers to thought questions are not directly found in the text. They are not meant to be hard, but they can be if one lacks an adequate Bible background. They can be skipped as needed.

Application Questions
Usually at the end, though sometimes scattered in the middle of the Biblical questions, are application questions. These questions will encourage you to ask, "How is this passage relevant to my life?" These answers are meant to be personal and will have to do with your own life. It may take a little more time to properly work through these questions, but this is where you will begin to integrate the truth with your Christian life.

Advanced Questions

Advanced questions are designed for the astute student who wants to delve deeper into the truths of God's Word. Advanced students will have already been trained to study other parts of the scriptures and can relate a broader Biblical perspective to the passage. Some of these passages are so rich and deep that a simple Bible study cannot capture the many truths therein. These questions tend to be more applicative both in a practical and theological sense. They are designed to allow God's Word to reshape your thoughts and firm up your commitments.

In the basic set of questions, we focus on what is being said directly and teach you how to simply apply that lesson to your life; however, in the advanced set of questions, we will walk you through a deeper analysis of the text using the given study questions. And though they tend to require more time, these questions better flesh out the meaning and purpose of the passage. We suggest the Bible study leader to go through these first to have a firmer grasp on the passage's purpose.

Leading Bible Studies

If you are using these questions in your small group Bible study time, we have some suggestions on how to move through them. Generally, the questions go from the beginning of the selected passage and proceed, verse by verse, until the end.

Sometimes the answer to a future question comes up in a question discussed previously. We suggest you skip it rather than repeat it. In fact, be ready to skip any question that seems not to go where the Spirit of God is leading the study. Often, the Spirit directs us toward a certain emphasis, such as, for example, how to practically love those who hurt you. Be alert and spend more time on that theme even if it requires that you skip over other questions. Prior to the study, be familiar with all the questions, including the advanced questions, so you are at liberty to jump around as needed. Never feel compelled to finish all the questions. Every study is different, and so is the time allotted for each study. Remember, our goal is to uncover and release the power of God's truth rather than to mention every question! In light of this goal, go through the questions and mark the ones you are considering for use. And, of course, feel free to add your own questions if they are a fit for the occasion!

TABLE OF CONTENTS

Usage of Study Questions — 5

An Introduction to 1 Peter — 11

1 Peter 1:1-2 Study Questions — 19
- An Introduction — 19
- Advanced Questions — 22

1 Peter 1:3-12 Study Questions — 25
- The Rich Hope of Salvation — 25
- Advanced Questions — 30

1 Peter 1:13-22 Study Questions — 33
- Contending with a Spirit of Compromise — 33
- Advanced Questions — 38

1 Peter 1:22-2:3 Study Questions — 39
- God's Word Alive in Us — 39
- Advanced Questions — 44

1 Peter 2:4-10 Study Questions — 45
- The Chosen People of God — 45
- Advanced Questions — 50

1 Peter 2:11-25 Study Questions — 53
- Respect for All — 53
- Advanced Questions — 59

1 Peter 3:1-7 Study Questions — 61
- Marriage Advice! — 61
- Advanced Questions — 66

1 Peter 3:8-12 Study Questions — 69
- Our Godly Heritage — 69
- Advanced Questions — 74

1 Peter 3:13-22 Study Questions — 75
Suffering for Righteous Causes — 75
Advanced Questions — 80

1 Peter 4:1-6 Study Questions — 81
Living for God's Will — 81
Advanced Questions — 85

1 Peter 4:7-11 Study Questions — 87
Accomplishing the Will of God — 87
Advanced Questions — 90

1 Peter 4:12-19 Study Questions — 91
The Right Way to Suffer — 91
Advanced Questions — 96

1 Peter 5:1-4 Study Questions — 97
Developing Godly Leadership — 97
Advanced Questions — 101

1 Peter 5:5-7 Study Questions — 103
Serving under Church Leadership — 103
Advanced Questions — 108

1 Peter 5:8-14 Study Questions — 109
Final Advice for the Believers — 109
Advanced Questions — 115

Appendix #1: About the Author — 116

LIVING HOPE IN A FALLEN WORLD
1 Peter

An Introduction to 1 Peter

¹Peter, an apostle of Jesus Christ, to those who reside as aliens, scattered throughout Pontus, Galatia, Cappadocia, Asia, and Bithynia, who are chosen ²according to the foreknowledge of God the Father, by the sanctifying work of the Spirit, that you may obey Jesus Christ and be sprinkled with His blood: May grace and peace be yours in fullest measure (1 Peter 1:1-2).

Circumstances could not be much worse: kicked out of their homes, suffered loss of work, and removed from friends and family. Peter the apostle calls these scattered Christians to imitate Jesus' path of service in faithfulness, suffering, and glory.[1] By closely following the resurrected Christ, believers found the extra strength to keep them in a dark and desperate world—not just by appearances also but deep down in their hearts; if people scoffed at them or if their possessions were taken, their hearts could yet be filled with Christ's joy.

Outline for 1 Peter

Peter sent comfort and encouragement to the believers who were scattered, due to oppressive situations, so that they could live strong and godly lives. By learning how to conduct ourselves as the chosen people of God, we can live vibrant Christ-filled lives in this dark and often hostile world.

✦ Introduction (1:1-2) – An Unexpected Encounter

---

[1] Isaiah's Servant Song (Isaiah 52:13-53:12) has earlier revealed this path. For an in-depth study see: www.foundationsforfreedom.net/Topics/ADT/Courses/Isaiah-ADT0-52.13-53.12_Leadership.html

Peter seeks God's fullest measure of blessing in the lives of the Christian believers, who were scattered from their homes, by reminding them that they belonged to God.

✣ A) A Precious Calling (1:3-2:10)
Embrace our calling to live out holy lives

By focusing our minds on our glorious inheritance in Christ and on our precious faith, we affirm our calling and further strengthen our belief and commitment to fulfilling Christ's purpose for our lives.

✣ B) A Holy Lifestyle (2:11-3:12)
Live godly lives to help others know Christ

As God's holy people, we are to embrace our positions and callings in this world, be they low or high, and to conduct holy lives so that others who hold to different beliefs might come to know God.

✣ C) A Christ-like Heart (3:13-5:11)
Honorably endure suffering to receive a crown of glory

By catching a glimpse of Jesus' life when He faced trials, we can find strength to use during our short time on earth to endure suffering so that we can obtain that imperishable crown of glory.

✣ Conclusion (5:12-14)

Peter summarizes his purpose in a general way at the end of the book, "I have written to you briefly, exhorting and testifying that this is the grace of God" (5:12). He encouraged God's people to see God actively working in and through their oppressive situations.

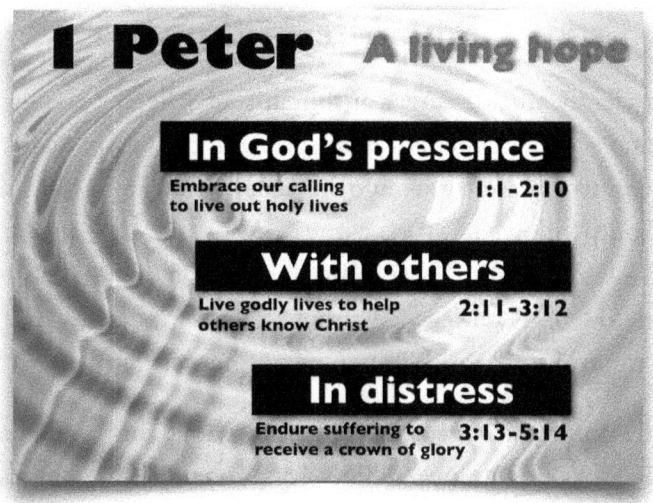

Key words and Themes

Below we have gathered some key words in 1 Peter based on their frequency of appearance (words on the left are more common): God, Jesus, suffer, glory, grace, love, holy, sin, and reveal. As a bonus exercise look for each of these words or synonyms as you read through 1 Peter.

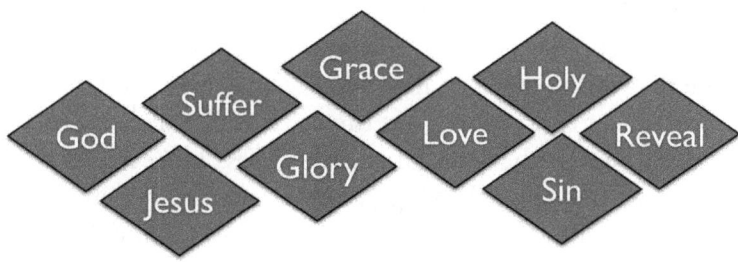

Peter the Author

The letter clearly affirms Peter's authorship of 1 Peter, leaving no reason to question it. Peter's experiences, as shared in the Gospels and the Book of Acts, confirm his insights and help us better appreciate this book. Peter not only followed Christ, witnessed His miracles, and heard Jesus' teachings but also had to learn to live by faith when Jesus was no longer by His side. Here, Peter learned about trials, temptations, and suffering as well as the triumph of the church when she was faithful.

Peter's affection for Christ is evident throughout this book, both in the way he describes how Jesus regularly conducted His life but also in how He described Jesus' suffering and the cross. By trusting in God, Jesus accomplished a much greater good than otherwise could have been carried out. Once Peter moved to Rome (tradition), he oversaw the whole church but also faced martyrdom there during Nero's Christian persecution. Clement of Rome in his Epistle to Corinthians (don't confuse with the scripture book) said this of Peter and Paul,

> "Let us come to the heroes nearest to our times.... Let us set before our eyes the good apostles; Peter, who by reason of unrighteous jealousy endured not one or two but many labours, and having thus borne his witness went to his due place of glory. Paul, by reason of jealousy and strife, pointed out the prize of endurance.... When he had preached in the East and in the West he received the noble renown of his faith. Having taught righteousness to the whole world, even reaching the bounds of the West, and having borne witness before rulers, he thus left the world and went to the holy place, becoming the greatest pattern of endurance."[2]

As we reflect on what we know of Peter through the story of the gospels, these verses will spring to life.

---

[2] Documents of the Christian Church by Henry Bettenson, 2nd ed., p. 8.

The Scattered Flock

Peter wrote to Christian believers scattered over a number of districts: Pontus, Galatia, Cappadocia, Asia, and Bithynia (1:1). These districts now comprise the country of modern day Turkey. See if you can find them in the map below.

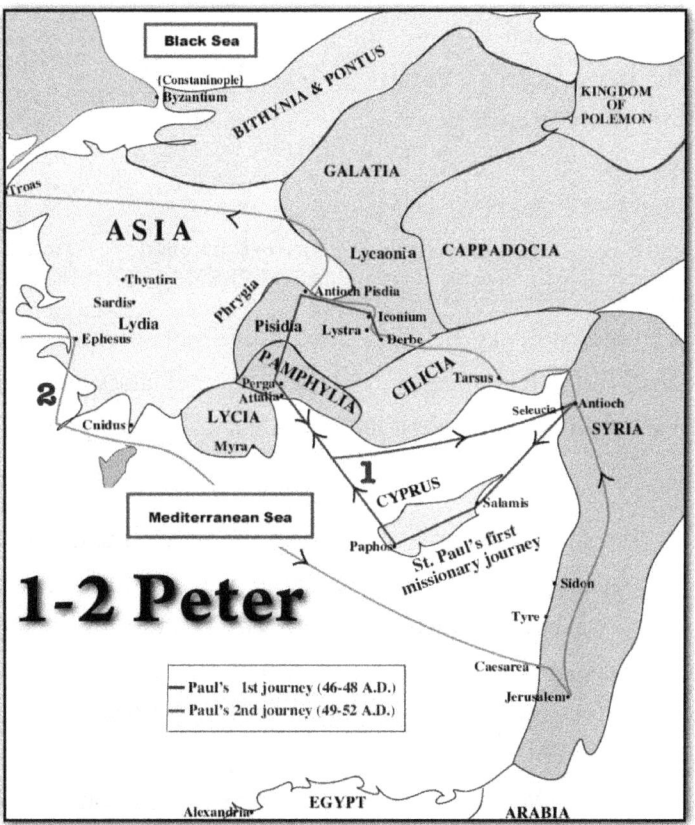

It is interesting to note that Paul's first and second journeys took him through parts of these areas. Peter was called the Apostle to the Jews but no doubt later, as tradition records, oversaw both Jews and Gentiles in Rome after Paul's martyrdom. He cared for the believers east of Rome in the aforementioned regions. His remains are said to be buried under St. Peter's Basilica in Rome.

Aliens but Chosen

The first verses of 1 Peter introduce the major themes of alien, chosen, and holy, which weave their way through 1 Peter. Peter first describes his audience as "aliens" (verse 1). This word, along with the adjacent word "scattered," shows us that they were oppressed for their faith. The word "aliens" implies they did not choose their place of residence but, as refugees, had been driven out from their home and forced to settle elsewhere. Greater forces compelled them to leave their attachments behind—including their families, churches, possessions, and friends—and to enter strange lands with different languages, cultures, and worship, often experiencing poverty in the process.

Scattered	Chosen
random	deliberate
unimportant	important
aliens	key agents
lack resources	many resources
man-controlled	God-directed

Peter uses this alien concept to emphasize the biblical teaching of being chosen, the second theme word. The whole situation looked so random, almost as if God was not watching over them. From the Old Testament, we know the dangers of being thrown into other cultures (i.e., Canaan). God's people are susceptible to adopting their evil habits. But we also know of great exceptions including those holy—our last theme—people like Joseph and Daniel who lived out their righteousness in high positions of some of the world's greatest empires.

God chose these believers. Their circumstances were not unlike those of Peter, who was thrown into jail (Acts 4), and a "great persecution began against the church in Jerusalem, and they were all scattered throughout the regions of Judea and Samaria, except the apostles" (Acts 8:1). Peter is not condemning them for escaping but instead reminds them that God is able to keep His people during times of persecution. Formerly,

Peter denied Jesus, but this time he remained firm and faithfully served the flock of God.

The book of 1 Peter was probably written around 62 AD. When Nero, the emperor of the Roman empire, instigated a persecution against Christians, he falsely blamed a fire as being the fault of the believers and thus persecuted them. Later on during this period (62-64 AD), they also martyred Peter the Apostle in Rome. This would be well after Paul the Apostle's trips to this area in 46-52 AD and his own martyrdom.

Life Applications

Our importance in the world does not matter as much as being known to be faithful by God in Christ. By knowing Christ, we know that we not only belong to God forever but that He carefully watches over us during our trials.

Those who do not suffer in some way, shape, or form will face greater challenges to maintain a vibrant faith. The more one is established and esteemed by the world, the more challenging it is to maintain a greater regard of one's faith than one's position in the world, thus making it difficult for believers to possess a strong faith in comfortable times.

LIVING HOPE IN A FALLEN WORLD
1 Peter

1 Peter 1:1-2 Study Questions

An Introduction

¹Peter, an apostle of Jesus Christ, to those who reside as aliens, scattered throughout Pontus, Galatia, Cappadocia, Asia, and Bithynia, who are chosen ²according to the foreknowledge of God the Father, by the sanctifying work of the Spirit, that you may obey Jesus Christ and be sprinkled with His blood: May grace and peace be yours in fullest measure (1 Peter 1:1-2).

Peter sought to encourage the Christian believers, who were scattered from their homes, of God's fullest measure of blessing in their lives by reminding them that they belonged to God.

1. Based on your current Bible knowledge, list five scenes included in the Gospels and Acts in which Peter stood out as one of the major characters. List one of Peter's traits from each scene.

2. What is an alien? Why do you think he called them aliens (1:1)?

3. What places did Peter mention in 1 Peter 1:1? Locate them on a Biblical map. Find this same area on a modern map.

4. Peter also calls them "scattered." Do you think this means they were being oppressed and were refugees? Scan 1 Peter to confirm your answer.

5. Peter included many theological teachings in 1 Peter 1:1-2. Carefully go over these verses and state what main doctrines Peter introduced. State both the significant words and the associated teaching(s).

   -
   -
   -
   -

6. What does "chosen" refer to in 1 Peter 1:2? Who does the choosing? What are the implications of being chosen?

7. Who are the three persons Peter refers to in 1:2? From Peter's words, what is the relevance of each one to our lives?

8. Though the word "trinity" is not used in the Bible, do you think Peter here was subtly introducing the three persons of the trinity? Explain.

9. Throughout this book, Peter seeks ways to infuse God's "grace and peace" into their lives (1:2). How would you describe "grace" and "peace" in your own words? Which do you sense a greater need for right now?

10. When is one time you felt isolated or that you did not belong? What is one way God's persistent care for you helps affirm how much you belong to Him?

Advanced Questions

✦ While reading through the Gospel of Mark and Acts 1-12, highlight the things Peter experienced and learned. Note the significance of how these things might have shaped his faith and, by extension, this book.

✦ How did Peter's letter historically relate to Paul's missionary journeys? Suggestion: start by comparing the dates and places of Paul's journey, his martyrdom, and the possible date of this letter along with Peter's martyrdom.

✦ Do you think doctrine is important? Why or why not? Does your church think much of doctrine? Why do you think Peter emphasized doctrine so much in this book?

✦ Does the teaching of election and the use of this word "chosen" here refer to the same thing? Explain. Why is it important to know one is chosen (Peter thought it was important)?

✦ Pick two of the following teachings gleaned from 1 Peter 1:1-2. Summarize the teaching and discuss why each teaching is important to our lives as believers.

➡ 'One God in three persons'

- Chosen according to foreknowledge of God the father

- Sanctifying work of the Spirit

- Being sprinkled with Christ's blood

LIVING HOPE IN A FALLEN WORLD
1 Peter

1 Peter 1:3-12 Study Questions

The Rich Hope of Salvation

Christian believers learn how their faith in Christ helps them embrace God's abounding grace to gain their eternal award no matter what they might face. Peter identifies four hopes that verify the extraordinary value of our faith in Christ.

(1) A Sure Hope (1:3)

God's miraculous work in a believer's life begins with spiritual birth, which gives new life that is enabled through the resurrection of Jesus Christ.

> ³Blessed be the God and Father of our Lord Jesus Christ, who according to His great mercy has caused us to be born again to a living hope through the resurrection of Jesus Christ from the dead (1 Peter 1:3).

1. State in your own words the meaning of "Blessed be" (1:3).

2. What two reasons does Peter give us to bless God in verse 3?

3. What does it meant to "be born again?" Read John 3:1-8 for further understanding.

4. What does the resurrection of Jesus Christ have to do with living hope?

5. Do you think that you deserve salvation? Explain. How does your answer match up with the concept that it is by the mercies of God (1:3) that one is saved?

(2) An Eternal Hope (1:4)

God's intention is that each new life would spring up and keep blossoming into eternity.

> ⁴To obtain an inheritance which is imperishable and undefiled and will not fade away, reserved in heaven for you (1 Peter 1:4).

6. What is an inheritance? What inheritance will they and you gain (Eph 1:11,14,18; Col 1:12; Heb 9:15; 11:8)? When?

7. List the three descriptions of this inheritance found in verse 4. How are they different from each other?

8. What part of verse 4 do you like the most and why?

(3) An Enduring Hope (1:5-7)

God gives us a hope that continues through bad times. Though Satan tempt us, the world lure us, and our flesh battle us, God's power is stronger. We might not feel like holding on, but we do and we must.

> ⁵Who are protected by the power of God through faith for a salvation ready to be revealed in the last time. ⁶In this you greatly rejoice, even though now for a little while, if necessary, you have been distressed by various trials, ⁷that the proof of your faith, being more precious than gold which is perishable, even though tested by fire, may be found to result in praise and glory and honor at the revelation of Jesus Christ (1 Peter 1:5-7).

9. A number of things that threatened their faith were mentioned in this passage. List the ones found here and complement this list with other possible threats to their faith.

10. It is good that the power of God protects us! But how does it accomplish protection? Take one or two of the items from the former list and state how God's power makes a difference in those situations.

11. Describe the imagery used by the phrase "tested by fire" (1:7).

12. What does "at the revelation of Jesus Christ" refer to (1:7)? Also, compare Acts 1:9-11 and 1 Peter 1:13, 4:13.

13. Do you ever fear the loss of your faith or wonder if it is strong enough to withstand the trials that might come? Explain.

(4) A Genuine Hope (1:8-12)

God's protection of our eternal salvation is found in our faith, that, though tested, will endure and bring grand praise upon Christ's return.

> ⁸And though you have not seen Him, you love Him, and though you do not see Him now, but believe in Him, you greatly rejoice with joy inexpressible and full of glory, ⁹obtaining as the outcome of your faith the salvation of your souls."
>
> ¹⁰As to this salvation, the prophets who prophesied of the grace that would come to you made careful search and inquiry, ¹¹seeking to know what person or time the Spirit of Christ within them was indicating as He predicted the sufferings of Christ and the glories to follow. ¹²It was revealed to them that they were not serving themselves, but you, in these things which now have been announced to you through those who preached the gospel to you by the Holy Spirit sent from heaven--things into which angels long to look" (1 Peter 1:8-12).

14. How do they express their faith (1:8)? Who does "him" refer to in this verse? What makes you think so?

15. Verse 9 states that our enduring faith results in the salvation of our souls. What is a soul and what does the verse mean by "salvation of your souls?"

16. What did the prophets of old seek to know? What did they discover (1:10-12)?

17. How do the Old Testament prophets help clarify things more for us in the New Testament age than for the prophets themselves (10-11)?

18. Why do you think the angels long to look into these things (1:12)?

19. How true is it of you that you "love Him" and "believe in Him" (1:9) though you do not see Him?

Advanced Questions

- Peter states "resurrected from the dead" in verse 1:3. Incipient forms of Gnosticism were found during this time. They would generally deny that Christ had a body and therefore He could not die. They believed the body was evil (much like believers of Hinduism, Buddhism, and other forms of Eastern mysticism). How would the emphasis "from the dead" combat this distorted view of the human body? What is the correct view?

- Compare Paul's (Eph 1:3) and Peter's (1:3) "Blessed...." phrases in the scriptures.

- Verse 4 speaks about our eternal inheritance. Do you meditate much on this? Set aside at least ten minutes and think up ten great things about this eternal inheritance.

- Peter speaks to how the power of God protects our faith. In light of this passage, how do you explain those who lose their faith or just don't care for their faith anymore?

- When Peter was writing, the New Testament was not yet fully collected. Different books like this were written to various areas. The Old Testament was fully formed, however, and had a great impact on believers as it still does today. What are some things we learn about the prophets and the Old Testament scriptures from 1 Peter 1:10-12? Try to answer questions like, "Who wrote them?" "Why did they write them?" "What did the authors know about their purpose?" "Did they believe there was something greater coming?" "What did they know about the greater One or thing?" "How should we in the gospel era be helped by these sacred books?"

- From these verses, what would you say is the best way to protect and strengthen your faith? How will you make sure those things are practiced in your life? Be practical and follow up on yourself.

Living Hope in a Fallen World
1 Peter

1 Peter 1:13-22 Study Questions

Contending with a Spirit of Compromise

Compromise dulls our Christian lives. Peter faced this problem, and so will we. Peter lists three ways to strengthen ourselves to challenge this spirit of compromise.

(1) By Our Future Hope (1:13)

¹³Therefore, gird your minds for action, keep sober in spirit, fix your hope completely on the grace to be brought to you at the revelation of Jesus Christ (1 Peter 1:13).

1. What are the things in the previous verses that lead Peter to say "therefore" at the beginning of this verse (1:3-13)?

2. How many commands does Peter give us in this verse? List them below:

    ❖

    ❖

    ❖

3. In your own words, how would you write the first command in the list?

4. What does "sober in spirit" mean?

5. Read about Peter's sleepiness and its ramifications in Matthew 26:42-46. How might this verse relate to Peter's experience?

6. Explain what grace means in verse 13 and in what way it is connected with Jesus' second coming?

7. Do you tend to be hopeful or easily discouraged? Have you ever pondered upon how things might be like after Jesus returns? Try it for ten minutes!

(2) By Our Holy Conduct (I Peter 1:14-16)

¹⁴ As obedient children, do not be conformed to the former lusts which were yours in your ignorance, ¹⁵ but like the Holy One who called you, be holy yourselves also in all your behavior; ¹⁶ because it is written, "YOU SHALL BE HOLY, FOR I AM HOLY" (1 Peter 1:14-16).

8. What does the phrase "obedient children" refer to (1:14)?

9. List five lusts or strong desires that can grab hold of a person (1:14; also 4:2-3).

1 Peter 1:13-22 Study Questions

10. How is ignorance related to a wild lifestyle (1:14)?

11. We are to be holy like God. How is God holy? What does "holy" mean (1:15)?

12. In what way can we be holy like God (1:15)? Is it possible?

13. Where does Peter get the insight that we are to be holy like God (1:16)?

14. In what area is it most difficult for you to be holy like God?

(3) By Our Reverent Attitude (1:17-21)

"17And if you address as Father the One who impartially judges according to each man's work, conduct yourselves in fear during the time of your stay upon earth; 18knowing that you were not redeemed with perishable things like silver or gold from your futile way of life inherited from your forefathers, 19but with precious blood, as of a lamb unblemished and spotless, the blood of Christ. 20For He was foreknown before the foundation of the world, but has appeared in these last times for the sake of you 21who through Him are believers in God, who raised Him from the dead and gave Him glory, so that your faith and hope are in God" (1 Peter 1:17-21).

15. For what reasons might God be called "Father" (1:17)?

16. Is Peter trying to convey either that the Father is like a Judge and that we should fear Him or that God acts as both a Father and a Judge (1:17)?

17. What does redeemed mean (1:18)? Try to think of an instance where you might hear the word "redeem" or "redemption" used today?

18. What cannot redeem a person? What does it take to redeem a person (1:18-19)?

19. Why is Christ compared to "a lamb unblemished and spotless" (1:19)?

20. What does it mean that Jesus was "foreknown before the foundation of the world" (1:20)?

21. How is it that we "are believers in God" through Jesus (1:21)?

22. How is the resurrection relevant to our faith (1:21)?

23. Are you a believer in the God of the Scripture? Why? When did you become "saved" or what is it that keeps you from fully believing in Christ?

Summary

Believers live beyond what they see on earth or even what they might feel in their desires. Christian disciples live by faith and are motivated by hope in God's redeeming work. As God's children, believers look forward to seeing their new home. Let's put away the ways of compromise and instead live by a fixed hope, holy conduct, and reverent attitude.

Advanced Questions

- We will never be able to make right decisions about money until we start living in light of tomorrow's grace. The life that is not ruled by faith in what is coming is shaped only by what one sees. Does your spending reflect this eternal hope? How so?

- Holiness is a very important biblical word. Look up the five times the word "holy" is used and discuss its development and usage in the church.

- Peter quotes, "Be holy for I am holy" from two places in the Old Testament. Look up each and find whom God is addressing in each case:

    - Leviticus 11:44:

    - Leviticus 19:2:

- Go through these verses and state all the things it says about Jesus Christ. Focus especially on the question, "Was Jesus ever created?" What does it mean that God foreknew Christ before the world began?

LIVING HOPE IN A FALLEN WORLD
1 Peter

1 Peter 1:22-2:3 Study Questions

God's Word Alive in Us

Our Christian life calls us to go beyond the world's love and to supernaturally love others God's way, but we need to realize this *agape* love comes from the new spiritual nature and strengthens our spiritual lives through God's Word to exercise it.

(1) Fervently Love One Another (1:22-25)

> 22Since you have in obedience to the truth purified your souls for a sincere love of the brethren, fervently love one another from the heart, 23for you have been born again not of seed which is perishable but imperishable, that is, through the living and abiding word of God. 24For, "ALL FLESH IS LIKE GRASS, AND ALL ITS GLORY LIKE THE FLOWER OF GRASS. THE GRASS WITHERS, AND THE FLOWER FALLS OFF, 25BUT THE WORD OF THE LORD ABIDES FOREVER." And this is the word which was preached to you (1 Peter 1:22-25).

To encourage the believers to move into a God-empowered love, Peter reveals the part God has in our salvation and in our spiritual growth.

1. Peter is speaking to the scattered believers. What might "Since you have in obedience to the truth" refer to (see 1:22a)?

2. What step in their Christian lives does "purified your souls for a sincere love of the brethren" might refer to (1:22b)?

3. What are the two kinds of loves mentioned in verse 22? What are the differences? (Hint: The Greek uses two different words: brotherly *philadelphia* love while the later uses devoted, *agape,* love.)

4. To what topic does Peter shift in verse 23?

5. What does it mean to be "born again" (also refer to 1:3)?

6. What do seeds do? How might seeds and being born again relate to each other?

7. What is the seed that brings spiritual life (1:23)?

8. How does Peter describe the Word of God (1:23-24)?

9. What is Peter describing in verse 24? Read the original verse and see whether you guessed correctly. Read Isaiah 40:6-8 carefully.

10. Why might Peter conclude this section with: "And this is the word which was preached to you" (1:25)?

11. Think of three relationships in your life. Would you describe your love as typical love or as God-empowered love? Why?

(2) Long for God's Word (2:1-3)

2:1<u>Therefore</u>, putting aside all malice and all guile and hypocrisy and envy and all slander, ²like newborn babes, long for the pure milk of the word, that by it you may grow in respect to salvation, ³if you have tasted the kindness of the Lord (1 Peter 2:1-3).

12. Note the use of "therefore" in 2:1. Remember that the original paragraphs are completely arbitrary. How does Peter connect these verses with what comes before it?

13. List the things Peter tells them to put aside (2:1). Describe each.

-

-

-

-

-

14. With which area do you struggle the most? Explain and, as applicable, tell the Lord that you will commit to "putting aside."

15. What life analogy is Peter using in verse 2:2? Explain it in your own words.

16. What spiritual truth does Peter highlight by using this analogy? How do you know?

17. How does Peter suggest that we can grow in our spiritual lives?

18. How do you use God's Word to grow in your life?

19. Why might Peter add those extra words in verse 3, "If you have tasted the kindness of the Lord?"

20. Conclusion: Peter wants our love to go beyond its present state. He knows, however, that our love can't reach the levels it needs to without the influence of God's powerful Word actively shaping our lives. Give a situation where you have found extra strength and purpose to use God's *agape* love to love someone. How did God's Word specifically help you to love that person?

Advanced Questions

- Give three incidents wherein you observed the frailty of a person.

- Are you born again? When and where? What circumstances surrounded your new birth?

- How is our new nature different from our old nature?

- After looking at all of these verses, how would you say that a person gains a spiritual life or nature?

- What might the "word of God" refer to? Try to identify one or two times when God "spoke" to you. Was it through the scriptures or some other way?

- List two verses or sections of scripture that God has used in the recent past to help you grow. How did He use them in your life?

LIVING HOPE IN A FALLEN WORLD
1 Peter

1 Peter 2:4-10 Study Questions

The Chosen People of God

Peter exhorts the scattered believers who had lost their earthly identities to affirm their privileged calling in relationship to the person and work of Christ Jesus. He also provides a description of the community of believers.

(1) A Living Stone (2:4-5)

If believers want to understand their lives, they must first come to understand the One who made and calls them. If there is any confusion at this basic level, then there is no hope for further clarity.

> ⁴And coming to Him as to a living stone, rejected by men, but choice and precious in the sight of God, ⁵you also, as living stones, are being built up as a spiritual house for a holy priesthood, to offer up spiritual sacrifices acceptable to God through Jesus Christ (1 Peter 2:4-5).

1. Who is the "Him" identified in verse 4? How do you know (2:4)?

2. What might be the difference between a living stone and a stone?

3. Think about these believers' situation. Why might Peter emphasize the last part of verse 4, "Rejected by men, but choice and precious in the sight of God?"

4. List a few reasons Peter might have called the believers "living stones" (2:5)?

5. Name the three special designations of the people of God in verse five. Describe each image.

   ✦

   ✦

   ✦

6. What responsibilities do you have as part of a spiritual priesthood?

7. What kind of spiritual sacrifices does the Lord want (also refer to Romans 12:1-2)?

8. On what basis are we able to do these things or function in this way?

9. Do you see yourself as part of the holy priesthood? Please explain.

(2) A Living Stone (2:6-8)

All that we have as believers is totally dependent upon the person and work of Jesus Christ. The more we believe and live out that belief, the greater our hope will be. Unbelief is our chief enemy.

> ⁶BEHOLD I LAY IN ZION A CHOICE STONE, A PRECIOUS CORNER stone, AND HE WHO BELIEVES IN HIM SHALL NOT BE DISAPPOINTED." ⁷This precious value, then, is for you who believe. But for those who disbelieve, "THE STONE WHICH THE BUILDERS REJECTED, THIS BECAME THE VERY CORNER stone," ⁸and, "A STONE OF STUMBLING AND A ROCK OF OFFENSE"; for they stumble because they are disobedient to the word, and to this doom they were also appointed" (1 Peter 6-8).

10. Read aloud Peter's quote from the Old Testament in verse 5 as he supports his former claim. What stands out to you? (Zion is another name for Israel.)

11. What is a cornerstone (2:6) and how does it relate to the church?

12. Finish the quote in 2:6, "And he who believes _____

_____."

13. Who is the precious stone for (2:7)? What contrast does he make in this verse?

14. Why do unbelievers "stumble" (2:8)?

15. To what were they appointed (2:8c)?

(3) God's People (2:9-10)

The church is the most glorious institution ever known because of her calling and designated glorious purpose.

> ⁹But you are A CHOSEN RACE, A royal PRIESTHOOD, A HOLY NATION, A PEOPLE FOR God's OWN POSSESSION, that you may proclaim the excellencies of Him who has called you out of darkness into His marvelous light; ¹⁰for you once were NOT A PEOPLE, but now you are THE PEOPLE OF GOD; you had NOT RECEIVED MERCY, but now you have RECEIVED MERCY (1 Peter 2:9-10).

16. What four descriptions does Peter use of the people of God in verse 9? Describe each one the best you can in your own words.

✦

✦

✦

1 Peter 2:4-10 Study Questions

✦

17. Which description do you like the best? Why?

18. What is the purpose God has for His people as said in verse 9?

19. What might the "darkness" mentioned in verse 9 refer to? Why?

20. Name five excellencies of the Lord (2:9)?

21. Why do you think Peter quotes Old Testament verses (cf. Hosea 2:23)?

22. Set aside 15 minutes to meditate on the excellencies of our Lord and how special He has treated His people. Respond with a time of adoration.

Advanced Questions

- The church in the West, and increasingly those affected by modernism, often think of their own individual lives and needs instead of focusing on the needs of the whole community and the purpose of our calling. How do you see yourself doing in this battle between individualism and community?

- As one of many living stones that comprise the church, how do you rate the way you adjust to those around you? (Think of a wall made of many stones.)

- Jesus Christ is the only way to God. Why are some so insistent that Jesus is not the only way? What do you believe or not believe about Jesus Christ?

- In 1:1-3, Peter talks about election. Here he speaks about the believers end. Why do some believers have a difficult time accepting the teaching of election? Does the unbeliever deserve a severe punishment? The believer? Does the believer choose this? Check out verse 8.

- Would you say verses 9-10 refer to a future age or the present one? Why? If the former, why is it that the church is not grasping the glory and associated responsibility to proclaim the Lord?

- Train yourself in proclaiming His light. How might you do this? What regular disciplines would help you regularly spread His gospel?

- Choose one or two churches that you are fairly well acquainted with. How clear are they on their true identity?

What shows this? How well does their purpose agree with God's purpose stated here in 1 Peter? How do they carry it out? How might they be neglecting their function?

LIVING HOPE IN A FALLEN WORLD
1 Peter

1 Peter 2:11-25 Study Questions

Respect for All

Believers live as aliens in this world; their set of values is wholly different. Their lives follow Christ's example: living in respectful submission to human authority, putting off what is evil, doing what is good, and entrusting ourselves to God who judges justly.

(1) Living God's Values (2:11-12)

As strangers in this world, believers of Christ are to maintain their Lord's kingdom values with the hope that others will also come to love the Lord.

> ¹¹Beloved, I urge you as aliens and strangers to abstain from fleshly lusts, which wage war against the soul. ¹²Keep your behavior excellent among the Gentiles, so that in the thing in which they slander you as evildoers, they may on account of your good deeds, as they observe them, glorify God in the day of visitation (1 Peter 2:11-12).

1. What are the various ways that Peter addresses the believers in verse 11?

2. What does Peter urge them to do in verse 11?

3. What does "abstain from fleshly lusts" mean (2:11)? How do these lusts wage war against the soul?

4. How is the phrase in verse 12, "Keep your behavior excellent" similar or dissimilar to what is stated in verse 10?

5. Why does he mention the Gentiles? Who are they?

6. What "fleshly lusts" do you battle most with? How can these verses help you successfully wage war against them?

(2) Submitting to God's Authorities (2:13-20)

Being in control of our life situations makes life much easier, but this is not the option believers had then or in many cases now. All believers need to subject themselves to the authorities God has placed over them.

> [13]Submit yourselves for the Lord's sake to every human institution, whether to a king as the one in authority, [14]or to governors as sent by him for the punishment of evildoers and the praise of those who do right. [15]For such is the will of God that by doing right you may silence the ignorance of foolish men. [16]Act as free men, and do not use your freedom as a covering for evil, but use it as bondslaves of God. [17]Honor all men; love the brotherhood, fear God, honor the king. [18]Servants, be submissive to your masters with all respect, not only to those who are good and gentle, but also to those who are unreasonable. [19]For this finds favor, if for the sake of conscience toward God a man bears up under sorrows when suffering unjustly. [20]For what credit is there if, when you sin and are harshly treated,

you endure it with patience? But if when you do what is right and suffer for it you patiently endure it, this finds favor with God (1 Peter 2:13-20).

7. There is a key verb found in 2:13 that shapes how believers ought to live out their Christian lives. What is it? Write a few synonyms for this word.

8. Write down all the authorities to whom believers are told to subject themselves (2:13-14). Does this make sense?

9. What does Peter say the "will of God" is (2:15)? What advantage does observing God's ways have (2:15)?

10. Although we are under authority, we are to act as

    _____ (2:16). What does this mean?

11. Peter calls the believers "bondslaves" at the end of verse 16. How does this relate to subjecting oneself? Do you think they were really slaves or just servants of Christ?

12. What four general commands are mentioned in verse 17? Which ones apply to you? How so? Why might the other ones not apply?

13. What is the special command given to slaves of the time (2:18)?

14. What is the hardest requirement for slaves (2:18)?

15. How does Peter encourage the weak-hearted to completely live by God's ways in verses 19-20?

16. Describe the favor of God (2:20)? How important is it for you to secure this favor?

17. List your authorities and describe your willingness to submit to each one. What tension do you face? Do any of the instructions help? If so, how?

(3) Being Like Jesus in Suffering (2:21-25)

When we think of the call to follow Jesus, we do not often think of His example of suffering. Perhaps we do not suffer enough to pay attention to this detail, but for those who are suffering, Christ's example can powerfully encourage the hope and faith of those who have to put up with the mistreatment from others.

> 21For you have been called for this purpose, since Christ also suffered for you, leaving you an example for you to follow in His steps, 22WHO COMMITTED NO SIN, NOR WAS ANY DECEIT FOUND IN HIS MOUTH; 23and while being reviled, He did not revile in return; while suffering, He uttered no threats,

but kept entrusting Himself to Him who judges righteously; ²⁴and He Himself bore our sins in His body on the cross, that we might die to sin and live to righteousness; for by His wounds you were healed. ²⁵For you were continually straying like sheep, but now you have returned to the Shepherd and Guardian of your souls" (1 Peter 2:21-25).

18. Who does the "you" refer to in verse 2:21? Can that be applied to believers today? Why or why not?

19. What purpose is being referred to in verse 21?

20. Who does Peter say that Christ suffered for (2:21)?

21. Have you ever though about how Christ's suffering is an example to follow? Discuss.

22. Go through verses 22-23 and list the various aspects of Christ's example of suffering.

23. What does the last one, "kept entrusting Himself to Him who judges righteously" mean? Rewrite it in your own words.

24. Verse 24 is a wonderful verse that summarizes important parts of the Gospel. Name the different ones mentioned. Elaborate on each one's significance.

25. What picture does Peter use in verse 25? Memorize this verse and share your favorite part of it.

26. Identify one or two of the most difficult situations you needed to endure. Apply Jesus' example of enduring suffering to complete God's perfect will to your situations. Write down a prayer where you commit yourself to doing this.

Advanced Questions

- Peter again addresses these believers as aliens and strangers to point out the conflicting values between God's kingdom and the world. Identify five different values that the world around you has. How well do you maintain God's values?

- What is your experience when you choose to live countercultural (2:11-12)? Do you have extra opportunities to share the Gospel? Explain.

- The concept of submission today does not conjure up godly living but abuse. Why? What is the proper perspective? How is abuse different from Peter's advice *"patiently endure it?"*

- Think of those who do not submit to others. What happens to the culture when authority is not respected? Are there examples of this in your society?

- Sometimes, people use the phrase "for by His wounds you were healed" to refer to physical problems. What do you think it means? Refer to Isaiah 53:4-5 and Psalm 147:3.

- Limited or determined atonement refers to the teaching that Christ died for the sins of the genuine believers rather than for everyone. Examine 1 Peter 2:21-25. Do you find Peter has any problem affirming Christ died only for believers? What differences do the two views hold?

LIVING HOPE IN A FALLEN WORLD
1 Peter

1 Peter 3:1-7 Study Questions

Marriage Advice!

Both Paul and Peter briefly wrote on marriage, implying that both wives and husbands need good advice! Nothing has changed through the centuries. Marriages can go bad now just as they did back then. The root problems of marriage are related to mankind's fall into sin, and so the gospel can make a tremendous difference in a marriage whether here in the West or in various cultures across the globe. To the degree husbands and wives observe these biblical principles, marriages will thrive; but the opposite is equally true. When these principles are broken and self-interests persist, marriages will greatly suffer and bring much pain to all.

(1) Advice for Wives (3:1-6)

Peter calls wives to focus on two inner qualities to diminish the natural tendency for them to control and domineer their husbands.

> 3:1In the same way, you wives, be submissive to your own husbands so that even if any of them are disobedient to the word, they may be won without a word by the behavior of their wives, 2as they observe your chaste and respectful behavior. 3And let not your adornment be merely external--braiding the hair, and wearing gold jewelry, or putting on dresses; 4but let it be the hidden person of the heart, with the imperishable quality of a gentle and quiet spirit, which is precious in the sight of God. 5For in this way in former times the holy women also, who hoped in God, used to adorn themselves,

being submissive to their own husbands. ⁶Thus Sarah obeyed Abraham, calling him lord, and you have become her children if you do what is right without being frightened by any fear (1 Peter 3:1-6).

1. What does the phrase "in the same way" in verse 1 refer to?

2. Who is Peter addressing in these verses, and what does he instruct them to do in this first verse?

3. Are wives to be submissive when their husbands are not kind? How do you know (3:1)? Why doesn't it matter if they are believers or not? Explain.

4. In what way are husbands to be won over by their wives (3:1)?

5. How does verse 2 state that the husbands are affected by their wives' behavior?

6. How would you describe the words "chaste and respectful" behavior (3:2)?

7. What are some examples of outward adornment given in verse 3?

8. List the required qualities for wives (3:4). What does it mean that they are precious in the sight of God?

9. What does Peter refer to in verse 5 to strengthen his exhortation?

10. What did the women of old adorn themselves with (3:5)?

11. How is Sarah a good example (3:6)? What is the result if they follow her example?

12. How might fear enter these situations?

13. How do you or your spouse respond to this command? (If you're not married, consider your relationship with your parents.)

(2) Advice for Husbands (3:7)

The husband likewise has a responsibility to his wife. He is to kindly understand and live with his wife. Husbands are given two outstanding commands when it comes to their relationships with their wives: be understanding and give honor.

⁷You husbands likewise, live with your wives in an understanding way, as with a weaker vessel, since she is a woman; and grant her honor as a fellow heir of the grace of life, so that your prayers may not be hindered (1 Peter 3:7).

14. Why might the word "likewise" added here in verse 7?

15. What meaning does the phrase "in an understanding way" add to the command to the husbands?

16. Peter says men are to treat their wives as weaker vessels (3:7). How would that practically work out? Provide at least four examples.

17. Why should the husband treat his wife more gently (3:7)?

18. What might Peter mean by "a fellow heir of the grace of life" (3:7)? How would one practically honor his wife with this in mind?

19. What will happen if a man does not properly honor his wife (3:7)? What are the implications of this failure?

20. How do you or your spouse respond to this command? (If you're not married, consider your relationship with your parents.) What are the results of your situation?

Summary

Wives' vulnerability is actually their strong point when they understand and embrace the spiritual principle of submission. Husbands can spiritually grow and effectively serve only as they kindly treat and value their wives.

Advanced Questions

- Reflect and discuss how belief in the theory of evolution affects marriage; consider the differences between the following two views:

    (1) Men and women equally arose from the evolutionary chain, so no one can say that either men or women should rule or what marriage should look like.

    (2) In the Biblical account, God has designed and first created man and then woman as his helpmate. The roles are defined quite clearly.

- How has the feminist movement persuaded wives (and husbands) that it is best not to submit to their husbands? How do you or those around you deal with this popular perspective?

- Reflect upon the fall of mankind and the usurping spirit of women described in Genesis, "Yet your desire will be for your husband" (Gen 3:16). Would it be right to state that, because of this strong desire from the sinful nature, women are prone to reject the natural state of quiet submission?

- The Lord similarly seems to identify the root problem of men in Genesis 3:16 by the way they lead their wives, "Yet he will rule over you." Many believe this speaks not just to the husband's duty to govern the relationship but also assumes that they will do this in a despotic and authoritarian way. Do you find that husbands at times do not care to understand their wives and thus fall into an authoritarian style of leadership? Might this be identified by their violent bursts of anger?

- ✦ In many societies, men think it is okay to not kindly treat and honor their wives. What kind of changes need to practically take place so that the husbands kindly deal with their wives?

- ✦ Verse 3 does not include the word "merely." Why do women seem to especially have this problem with adornment? Christian groups have differing perspectives on outward adornment. What is your perspective? Does it meet up with the standards? Why or why not?

- ✦ What is your church doing to help married couples understand and conform to these good standards that Peter mentions? Discuss whether or not you believe that what Peter says is best. Why or why not?

LIVING HOPE IN A FALLEN WORLD
1 Peter

1 Peter 3:8-12 Study Questions

Our Godly Heritage

The source of the believer's power is his calling to be a blessing. The Christian brings the blessing of God to wherever he or she goes! No matter how wretched, dark, or discouraging the situation, the believer brings glory to God by helping others see the wonder of God's goodness through their life and words.

✦ Starter question: "Who aggravates you the most? Why?"

(1) Our Way to Live (3:8)

Lift the standard

⁸To sum up, let all be harmonious, sympathetic, brotherly, kindhearted, and humble in spirit; ⁹not returning evil for evil, or insult for insult" (1 Peter 3:8-9a).

1. "Finally" is a more accurate translation than to "sum up." What were the former points and how does this one differ from them (3:8)?

2. Define harmonious and sympathetic.

3. What is the difference between brotherly and kindhearted (3:8)?

4. What is "humble in spirit?" Is there any difference between this and simple humility?

5. What is the difference between "not returning evil for evil" and "insult for insult" (3:9a)?

6. Peter probably mentioned these virtues rather than others because he was thinking of their particular needs as refugees. Go back through the list and see if you can think how these characteristics might focus more on what these believers are facing.

7. Which area is easiest for you to handle? Which is the most difficult?

8. Do you think you can carry out the acts of kindness to which Peter calls you? Do you make excuses for yourself? How can you now live in kindness, especially with those who are difficult?

(2) Our Purpose to Live (3:9)

Identify the need

⁹But giving a blessing instead; for you were **called** for the very **purpose** that you might inherit a blessing (1 Peter 3:9).

9. What is he contrasting when he says, "<u>But</u> giving a blessing <u>instead</u>" (3:9)?

10. Is it wrong to wish evil upon those who have done evil to you? Why or why not?

11. Think through three practical ways you have given blessings in the past week.

12. Peter uses two keys words in verse 9: called and purpose. How are they related?

13. Do you think of your calling? How are you responsibly handling this special blessing?

14. Are you blessed so that you can enrich the lives of those around you or are you empty? Seek the Lord for His fullness!

15. Seek God for at least one person you can bless each day through encouraging words, kind actions, forgiving heart, financial or emotional support, a ride, a good word, etc.

(3) Our Reason to Live (3:10-12)

Kindly treat others

> ¹⁰For, "Let him who means to love life and see good days refrain his tongue from evil and his lips from soaking guile. ¹¹And let him turn away from evil and do good; let him seek peace and pursue it. ¹²For the eyes of the Lord are upon the righteous, and his ears attend to their prayer, but the face of the Lord is against those who do evil" (1 Peter 3:8-12).

Below is the text from the Old Testament from which the above passage is taken.

> Who is the man who desires life, And loves length of days that he may see good? ¹³ Keep your tongue from evil, And your lips from speaking deceit. ¹⁴ Depart from evil, and do good; Seek peace, and pursue it. ¹⁵ The eyes of the LORD are toward the righteous, And His ears are open to their cry. ¹⁶ The face of the LORD is against evildoers, To cut off the memory of them from the earth (Psalm 34:12-16).

16. What are the first few questions in Psalm 34:12 asking?

17. Look at 1 Peter 3:10-11 and list the honorable choices that promise a good life.

1 Peter 3:8-12 Study Questions

18. How are the first two phrases found in Psalm 34:13 different (or are they the same): "Keep your tongue from evil" and "[Keep] your lips from deceit"?

19. Are the two phrases from Psalm 34:14 the same or different?

    + Depart from evil and do good.

    + Seek peace and pursue it.

20. Psalm 34:15 clearly states that the eyes (or favor) of the Lord are toward the righteous. Some believers think this speaks about Christ's bestowed righteousness. But is this what the advice hints of? Discuss. (Is it righteousness through faith or in deeds that the Lord is looking for?) What difference does it make?

21. Whose prayer does the Lord hear (Psalm 34:15)? How does this compare with James 5:16-18?

22. How willing are you to equate a good life with these things rather than a good education or fortune? Discuss.

23. From reading these verses and observing the conclusion, what would you say the Lord thinks about a believer who is caught up in evil (3:16)? What advice could we give them?

Advanced Questions

- Do you live a life characterized by godly character? What areas can you improve on? Are there areas that you have ignored or justified and need to repent from? Take the necessary steps to reconcile yourself.

- Do you think by "inherit a blessing" Peter refers to blessings you have received or will yet receive? Explain. (Reflect on the possibility that the blessing is ours in Christ and yet its future richness is dependent on how we live.)

- God's promised blessings to Abraham's seed (Gen 12:1-3) seeks an outlet through our lives. Compare how God's former promises compare with what God is doing through His Church.

- Peter's confidence in the Old Testament was similar to Jesus' or Paul's confidence. We can learn from the sacred texts and discover answers! Do you believe the Old Testament text is reliable? Discuss.

- Does God's blessing go out to all of the justified (i.e., Christians) or is it dependent on the faithfulness of the way they live out their lives? How do you wrestle with this issue and keep this text in perspective?

- Write out and memorize the three steps that can be used to cope with temptation (see the lesson). Explain each and how it relates to the three scripture passages from 1 Peter 3:8-12.

LIVING HOPE IN A FALLEN WORLD
1 Peter

1 Peter 3:13-22 Study Questions

Suffering for Righteous Causes

Peter calls God's people to withstand suffering even while living a righteous life because God will surely use the evil to bring about a greater good.

(1) A Faithful Life (3:13-17)

Why do believers suffer? We might not find complete answers to this question, but nevertheless, we need to be ready to suffer as needed for Christ's Name. Peter's advice is priceless.

> ¹³And who is there to harm you if you prove zealous for what is good? ¹⁴But even if you should suffer for the sake of righteousness, you are blessed. AND DO NOT FEAR THEIR INTIMIDATION, AND DO NOT BE TROUBLED, ¹⁵but sanctify Christ as Lord in your hearts, always being ready to make a defense to everyone who asks you to give an account for the hope that is in you, yet with gentleness and reverence; ¹⁶and keep a good conscience so that in the thing in which you are slandered, those who revile your good behavior in Christ may be put to shame. ¹⁷For it is better, if God should will it so, that you suffer for doing what is right rather than for doing what is wrong (1 Peter 3:13-17).

1. What are the various reasons people suffer? Read 3:13. What kind of suffering is Peter addressing in this section?

2. How would you answer the question that Peter poses here in 3:13: "Who is there to harm you if you prove zealous for what is good?"

3. Being "zealous for what is good" is a great description of the believer. Give an example of how you can specifically work that out in your life.

4. Is it true that those who strive to be good will never suffer (3:14)? List three examples from the Bible that support your answer.

5. What is true of the righteous believer who unjustly suffers (3:14)? Read Matthew 5:10-12. How does what Jesus say compare with Peter's words?

6. Peter tells those who suffer for good should not fear their intimidators or oppressors (3:14-15). What should they do instead (3:15)? What does it mean to "sanctify Christ as Lord in your hearts?" How does this help them in those situations?

7. Have you ever suffered when doing something good and right? Please share. How did you respond to your oppressors?

8. What does it mean to "keep a good conscience" before such slanderers? Why is this piece of advice important (3:16)?

9. Does the phrase, "if God should will it so, that you suffer…" (3:17) mean that God sometimes permits believers to suffer?

10. We cannot control persecution; it happens to us. Verse 17 speaks about a choice though. What choice is that? How do we go about making that choice in those circumstances?

11. Have you ever thought about living an excellent life for Christ's glory? What practical way can you live a better life and sanctify Christ as Lord in your heart?

(2) A Persistence Hope (3:18-22)

Our hope for good to come out of evil comes from Christ and his example. Persecution, though, is one place where we cannot easily trace a good end result. We need to anticipate the fulfillment of God's greater purposes while we endure such circumstances.

> 18For Christ also died for sins once for all, the just for the unjust, in order that He might bring us to God, having been put to death in the flesh, but made alive in the spirit; 19in which also He went and made proclamation to the spirits now in prison, 20who once were disobedient, when the patience of God kept waiting in the days of Noah, during the construction of the ark, in which a few, that is, eight persons, were brought safely through the water. 21And

corresponding to that, baptism now saves you--not the removal of dirt from the flesh, but an appeal to God for a good conscience--through the resurrection of Jesus Christ, 22who is at the right hand of God, having gone into heaven, after angels and authorities and powers had been subjected to Him (1 Peter 3:18-22).

12. We might have trouble reconciling suffering and God's will, but notice whose suffering is mentioned in 3:18. What kind of suffering did he have to endure? List what is mentioned in this verse and five other acts of maltreatment.

13. While speaking of Christ's suffering, Peter goes on and speaks about the good that came from His death. What specific good does he mention in verse 18?

14. Explain the phrase "the just for the unjust" (3:18)?

15. Christ suffered by being put to death for us (3:18). Why did He need to die? What good did it bring about (3:18)?

16. Who proclaimed the gospel to the spirits in prison (3:19)? (Please note that these remaining verses have various interpretations, none very conclusive. We can try to understand them in connection to other passages, but remember not to form key teachings from them.)

17. Peter shows how good came from Christ's suffering by alluding to past events and people. Who or what symbol does he mention in verse 20? Verse 21?

18. How does Peter describe baptism in 3:21?

19. How does the resurrection of Jesus Christ connect to the concept and practice of baptism (3:21)?

20. Where is Jesus now (3:22)? What does this practically mean?

Summary

Good will always triumph over evil. Jesus Christ is the prime example of this as the one who went before us. We can gain confidence from this fact even when personally facing devastating acts of persecution.

Advanced Questions

- Peter clearly sees persecution taking place under the close scrutiny of the Lord. How do you reconcile the suffering of man with the love of God?

- It is possible that early forms of Gnostic teaching were around when Peter wrote this. The Gnostics believed that the body, the flesh, was evil and thus Christ could not really have had a human body. Note Peter's clarity, "having been put to death in the flesh but made alive in the spirit" (3:18). Have you met up with any similar Gnostic beliefs (similarities can be found in Hinduism and Christian Scientism in this sense). Explain.

- Jayasen, a good friend of mine with a similar passion to train up godly pastors was poisoned to death in his home in India. He was young and not yet married, but his life was wrongly cut short. List any evils against God's people that you know of.

- Read aloud Revelation 6:10 and cry out for those who have or are now suffering for their faith in Christ. What additional insight does Revelation 6:11 give to us?

- Read one or more chapters from *Fox's Book of Martyrs*.

- What are some situations in which you did good despite facing difficult people? What did you do?

1 Peter 4:1-6 Study Questions

Living for God's Will

In this set of study questions on 1 Peter 4:1-6, Peter highlights Christ's example by focusing on His determination, means, and purpose to live a godly life. Godly lives come by deliberate and consistent action. A spiritually empowered life does not come by passivity.

(1) Determining to live like Christ (4:1-2)

¹Therefore, since Christ has suffered in the flesh, arm yourselves also with the same purpose, because he who has suffered in the flesh has ceased from sin, ²so as to live the rest of the time in the flesh no longer for the lusts of men, but for the will of God (1 Peter 4:1-2).

1. Let's understand the meaning of verse 1. What are we commanded to do in verse 1?

2. Why are we told to do this (4:1)? What does this mean (note there are other possible interpretations of this phrase)?

3. How did Peter say that Christ suffered in 4:1? Expand what that might mean.

4. How is Peter's reminder of Christ's suffering supposed to motivate believers (4:1)?

5. What is the outcome of Jesus' decision not to live by the desires (lusts) of men (4:2)?

6. Distinguish the two opposing phrases in 1 Peter 4:2 by defining each of them:

   + Lusts of men

   + Will of God

7. Regarding this phrase in verse 1, "ceased from sin," is it possible to live a sinless life like Christ? How are we to apply this to our own lives?

8. What was your last sin? How have you lived by the "lusts of men"? How would life be different if you had lived by the will of God in those cases?

(2) Abstaining from our lusts (4:3-6)

³For the time already past is sufficient for you to have carried out the desire of the Gentiles, having pursued a course of sensuality, lusts, drunkenness, carousals, drinking parties and abominable idolatries. ⁴And in all this, they are surprised that you do not run with them into the same excess of dissipation, and they malign you; ⁵but they shall give account to Him who is ready to judge the living and the

dead. ⁶For the gospel has for this purpose been preached even to those who are dead, that though they are judged in the flesh as men, they may live in the spirit according to the will of God" (1 Peter 4:3-6).

9. How does Peter describe the ways of the Gentiles (literally meaning "nations")?

10. How would you describe the unbelievers' lives around you? Is it the same as described here? Describe.

11. Did you ever live with that mindset described in 4:3? What changed?

12. What are the people around believers surprised about in 4:4? Share at least one experience where you found this to be true with you—either with how you spoke or the things you did or did not do.

13. What reason do they and we have for not living as the world (4:5)?

14. Why might Peter differentiate the living from the dead in the coming of the great Judgment (4:5)?

15. Verse 4:6 links to verse 3:18. How does this relate to the materialists who view this life as a person's only existence?

16. Have you encountered those who strongly believe that this is the only life that we will experience? Who? What are your discussions like? Have you been able to bring up the topic of judgment? Explain.

17. Are there any areas of your life that you have not fully repented of? Which? Confess them now. Seek Christ's full forgiveness and make decisions to walk the life of Christ.

Summary

Peter points to the life of Jesus Christ. The world taunts us to join their party, but the oncoming seismic judgment demands that we completely focus on completing the will of God for our lives.

Advanced Questions

- As Mark's mentor, Peter had great influence on the writing of the Gospel of Mark. Mark 14:43-15 records the ways Jesus suffered. As time allows, note five ways Jesus suffered in the flesh (body). Which ones did Peter witness?

- Study the three interpretations of 1 Peter 4:6 ([see this resource](https://www.foundationsforfreedom.net/References/NT/Petrine/1Peter4-6_Interpretations.html)[3]). Which seems most plausible to you?

---

[3] https://www.foundationsforfreedom.net/References/NT/Petrine/1Peter4-6_Interpretations.html

LIVING HOPE IN A FALLEN WORLD
1 Peter

1 Peter 4:7-11 Study Questions

Accomplishing the Will of God

Believers have a limited time span to carry out God's appointed good works designated for their lives, and so they must lovingly learn how to use their spiritual gifts to accomplish God's significant purposes among God's people.

(1) Ready for God's Service (4:7-9)

⁷The end of all things is at hand; therefore, be of sound judgment and sober spirit for the purpose of prayer. ⁸Above all, keep fervent in your love for one another, because love covers a multitude of sins. ⁹Be hospitable to one another without complaint" (1 Peter 4:7-9).

1. What is fast approaching (4:7)? What does this mean?

2. How should this affect our lives (4:7)? See the two commands following the "therefore."

3. What does it mean to have a sound judgment (4:7)?

4. Restate the meaning of "sober spirit" in your own words. How can a sober spirit help a person's prayer life (4:7)?

5. What is the command given in 1 Peter 4:8? Why is this important (see the same verse)?

6. Why do you think Peter says "above all" in verse 8?

7. Describe the three spiritual ways of serving that are mentioned in 4:9,11.

8. What special advice does Peter give with each one of them (4:9,11)?

9. In what general context does Peter speak of spiritual gifts (see 4:8)? (For further study, note how Paul does the same thing in 1 Cor 12-14.)

(2) Carrying out God's Service (4:10-11)

¹⁰As each one has received a special gift, employ it in serving one another, as good stewards of the manifold grace of God. ¹¹Whoever speaks, let him speak, as it were, the utterances of God; whoever serves, let him do so as by the strength which God supplies; so that in all things God may be glorified through Jesus Christ, to whom

belongs the glory and dominion forever and ever. Amen" (1 Peter 4:10-11).

10. What are the general principles that we need to keep in mind as we use our spiritual gifts (4:10)?

11. What is the greater picture that we need to keep in mind as we serve the brethren (4:11)?

12. How do you practically serve the brethren? Can you honestly say that you show your love in the way you carry out your practical ministries?

Summary

You need three things to live a persistently strong Christian life: 1) Model your life after Jesus, who carefully lived out a prayerful life to carry out His Father's will; 2) increase your loving service to others; and 3) use your spiritual gifts as a means of displaying Jesus' love for the brethren.

Advanced Questions

+ Can a person just "happen" to live a godly life? Why or why not?

+ What commitment is God guiding you to focus on?

    + To God (4:7)?

    + To God's people (4:8)?

    + To God's service (4:9-11)?

    + Which of the above areas do you have most the difficulty with? Why?

+ What spiritual gift(s) do you have? How do you use it in your interactions with other believers?

+ How can you use these verses (4:7-11) to answer, "How can I know the will of God?"

LIVING HOPE IN A FALLEN WORLD
1 Peter

1 Peter 4:12-19 Study Questions

The Right Way to Suffer

It is neither normal nor strange for believers to have trials of faith. As God's Spirit rests upon us, we learn like other believers, to rejoice in our suffering on Christ's behalf while at the same time pressing on to do good.

(1) Suffering For God (4:12-16)

"12Beloved, do not be surprised at the fiery ordeal among you, which comes upon you for your testing, as though some strange thing were happening to you; 13but to the degree that you share the sufferings of Christ, keep on rejoicing; so that also at the revelation of His glory, you may rejoice with exultation. 14If you are reviled for the name of Christ, you are blessed, because the Spirit of glory and of God rests upon you. 15By no means let any of you suffer as a murderer, or thief, or evildoer, or a troublesome meddler; 16but if anyone suffers as a Christian, let him not feel ashamed, but in that name let him glorify God" (1 Peter 4:12-16).

A strong Christian must learn how to properly endure suffering and trials.

1. What is the main thing Peter wants to make clear in verse 12?

2. What major reason does Peter give to believers going through such trials (4:12)?

3. Are such difficult circumstances to be considered normal or exceptional (4:12)? Why?

4. What should our attitudes be toward this suffering (4:13)?

5. Believers can suffer in two ways. What are they (4:14-15)? What is the result of each?

   ❖

   ❖

6. What feelings might we face if we suffer as a Christians (4:16)? How is it suggested that we deal with them?

7. Share some stories about Christians suffering in the world today. (Check out the Voice of the Martyr website if you want to expand your knowledge: http://www.persecution.com.)

8. Have you ever suffered for doing <u>wrong</u>? What was it like? How is this different from suffering because you are a Christian believer?

(2) Suffering for the Believer (4:17-19)

¹⁷For it is time for judgment to begin with the household of God; and if it begins with us first, what will be the outcome for those who do not obey the gospel of God? ¹⁸AND IF IT IS WITH DIFFICULTY THAT THE RIGHTEOUS IS SAVED, WHAT WILL BECOME OF THE GODLESS MAN AND THE SINNER? ¹⁹Therefore, let those also who suffer according to the will of God entrust their souls to a faithful Creator in doing what is right" (1 Peter 4:17-19).

It is only when we have a Biblical understanding of trials that we will be equipped with the proper attitude to face suffering and persecution.

9. Who does the household of God refer to in 4:17?

10. What does Peter mean by, "It is time for judgment to begin with the household of God" (4:17)?

11. Why might Peter use the term "the household of God" (4:17)?

12. How does he refer to the unbelievers (4:17)?

13. What might "it is with difficulty that the righteous is saved" mean (4:18)? We know believers are not saved through their works, right (Eph 2:8-9)? Explain.

14. How would you answer the question Peter poses at the end of verse 18, "What will become of the godless man and the sinner?" How do you know?

15. Which of the two above groups (refer to question 5) does the phrase, "who suffer according to the will of God" refer to (4:19)? Why?

16. From Peter's description in verse 19, do you think it is ever right for God to allow His children to suffer?

17. What are two other ways to restate the phrase "entrust their souls" (4:19)?

18. What might Peter be alluding to when he emphasizes God as being a faithful Creator in this context (4:19)?

19. The scriptures clearly state in verse 19 that God does what is right. Do you ever think that God does anything not right? Explain.

20. Think about believers who are bitter about something. Do they think God doesn't handle situations justly? Why do you think this way? Is all bitterness related to not trusting God for doing what is good even in the worst of circumstances? Explain.

Summary

There are two levels of suffering: 1) The believer who suffers for doing what is right and 2) not being able to trust God in the suffering He might appoint. God can be fully trusted for any oppressive circumstances that believers face, and if we trust Him through these trials, we can much more easily trust Him for everything else we might face in life.

Advanced Questions

- How are people to "obey" the gospel of God (4:17)?

- Compare two sections of scripture in Titus and explain how they complement, rather than contradict, each other regarding the means of salvation: Titus 2:11-14 and 3:4-7.

- Many believers wrestle with the concept of an ongoing judgment of the unbeliever. Why? On what Biblical basis do others believe in eternal judgment? Include 2 Thessalonians 1:6-10 in your discussion.

- Are you bitter about something? How does that relate to your understanding of God's overall handling of the situation (e.g., having a wicked husband, ending up in debt, being unattractive, etc.). Confess any bitterness in your heart and trust God for all of your life circumstances into which God might lead you or others–even your loved ones. Read more on the last half of Romans 8 and suffering here.[4]

---

[4] https://www.foundationsforfreedom.net/References/NT/Pauline/Romans/Romans08/Romans08_18-25_Suffering.html

LIVING HOPE IN A FALLEN WORLD
1 Peter

1 Peter 5:1-4 Study Questions

Developing Godly Leadership

Peter has much to share about developing godly Christian leadership but keeps it direct and simple.

(1) Steps to Good Shepherding (5:1-3)

"¹Therefore, I exhort the elders among you, as your fellow elder and witness of the sufferings of Christ, and a partaker also of the glory that is to be revealed, ²shepherd the flock of God among you, exercising oversight not under compulsion, but voluntarily, according to the will of God; and not for sordid gain, but with eagerness; ³nor yet as lording it over those allotted to your charge, but proving to be examples to the flock" (1 Peter 5:1-3).

Peter had spent a lot of time at the feet of Jesus. He shares some of his many insights into godly leadership here in this brief passage.

1. What did Peter start doing in verse 1a? What does this mean?

2. What position did Peter have that he could "exhort elders" (5:1; cf. 1:1)? Name at least two things.

3. What might Peter be referring to when he speaks of "a partaker also of the glory that is to be revealed" (5:1)?

4. Who does the "flock of God" refer to (5:2)? Why might Peter use such a description?

5. Peter also uses the term "shepherd" to describe the process of caring for believers (5:2). Identify four or five verbs that describe what is needed to properly function as a shepherd of sheep (the people of God).

6. Who does Peter charge to shepherd the flock (5:1-2)? Who are these leaders in your church?

7. From verses 2-3, pick out three flaws in Christian leadership.

   ❖

   ❖

   ❖

8. Which problem area are you most sensitive to? Why?

9. What kind of situation develops when a leader exercises oversight under compulsion?

10. Do you think a lot of people serve in the church because of money (5:2)? Why would Peter say this?

11. List five ways you would want your Christian leaders to "prove to be examples to the flock" (5:3)?

12. What does it mean to "lord it over" those under one's charge (5:3)? What is the opposite?

13. Which of the above areas do you need to personally work on– even though you may not now be a leader?

Summary

There are good and poor Christian leaders. A poor leader discourages, whereas a good leader can inspire others to great good.

(2) Rewards for Faithful Shepherding (5:4)

> And when the Chief Shepherd appears, you will receive the unfading crown of glory (1 Peter 5:4).

Each Christian leader has the responsibility of serving the Lord now and the privilege of expecting a reward for that service in the future.

14. Who does Peter address in verse 4?

15. What does Peter promise them (5:4)?

16. What happens if they refuse to serve or serve poorly?

17. Who is the Chief Shepherd (5:4)? Why might Peter use this term?

18. For the pastors/elders, what are the implications of naming Jesus the Chief Shepherd?

Summary

Good leadership is truly something to be thankful for. But even if leaders are not performing well, we have direction from the scriptures to help us stay faithful to our Chief Shepherd.

Advanced Questions

- Some churches hold to a one-pastor or elder structure. How does this passage suggest a plural elder leadership group? What is the advantage of a group of godly leaders in the church?

- What is your experience with leaders from the church you attend now or those you've attended in the past?

- If you are a leader of a church, what is your greatest challenge?

- Does it help you as a member to know that Christ is the Chief Shepherd? Explain.

- How are Christians to handle impropriety among Christian leaders? Use biblical references to support your answer.

LIVING HOPE IN A FALLEN WORLD
1 Peter

1 Peter 5:5-7 Study Questions

Serving under Church Leadership

Every believer is either in leadership or under leadership. All of us are responsible to faithfully serve our Chief Shepherd wherever He calls us.

(1) The Call to Humility (5:5)

Peter takes us onto the path of humility, a place where none of us would like to go; yet Peter reminds us that greater blessings accompany us on this path and that we need not worry about anything.

> ⁵You younger men, likewise, be subject to your elders; and all of you, clothe yourselves with humility toward one another, for GOD IS OPPOSED TO THE PROUD, BUT GIVES GRACE TO THE HUMBLE (1 Peter 5:5).

1. What are the two groups Peter addresses in verse 5?

    ❖

    ❖

2. What command does the Apostle Peter give to younger Christian men (5:5)? Is it best to give such authority to leaders in today's church considering the abuse that can and does happen? Why or why not?

3. How is the second group—"and all of you"—connected to the first group (5:5)?

4. What does it mean "to clothe yourselves with humility toward one another" (5:5)? What are three practical ways to do this?

   ✣

   ✣

   ✣

5. Why does Peter say "likewise" to the younger men (5:5)?

6. What are the two key reasons Peter gives us this charge (5:5)?

   ✣

   ✣

7. Do you have trouble humbling yourself to those in authority over you? What is the most difficult part for you? Make sure you confess any hardening of your heart to your leaders.

Summary

Authority plays an important role in the local church. Verse 5 occurs subsequently to the former section (5:1-4) that speaks to the responsibilities that leaders have before the Lord. This verse reminds us, however, that it is equally important that those under leadership pay careful attention to how they serve their leaders.

(2) The Reward of Humility (5:6-7)

It's hard to be humble. When, however, we realize that humility leads to a far more fulfilling life, it is easier to deal with our arrogance and pride.

> ⁶Humble yourselves, therefore, under the mighty hand of God, that He may exalt you at the proper time, ⁷casting all your anxiety upon Him, because He cares for you (1 Peter 5:6-7).

8. Why might Peter add the phrase "under the mighty hand of God" when commanding them to "humble themselves" (5:6)?

9. What is the result of properly humbling oneself (5:6)?

10. What should we infer by the last words of verse 6: "at the proper time"?

11. How is disobedience related to pride?

12. Do you struggle with subjecting yourself to those in authority? Explain.

13. Memorize 5:7. What does verse 7 say about the anxiety we are to give to the Lord?

14. What illustration comes to your mind when you hear the phrase, "casting ... upon Him" (5:7)?

15. Why are we to trust Him with our worries (5:7)?

16. Peter transitioned from speaking about humbling oneself to putting aside anxiety. Why? How are they related?

17. What do you worry about most? If you really knew the Lord cared for you, would you worry? Explain.

Summary

Pride and anxiety are the two great enemies of the believer. Their presence indicates that we have somehow compromised our Christian lives. Humility is not based on doubt but on the confidence that God will always care for those who properly humble themselves under His care, leaving us no reason to worry.

Advanced Questions

- Today, more believers are rejecting the structured church and instead either avoid commitment to any one church or are establishing smaller house church networks. Why are believers doing this? What is the responsibility of each group before the Lord?

- Is it okay if all believers live without authority in the church? How can one serve the leadership if none claims to be in authority? Would our Chief Shepherd be happy with this?

- Why do some believers reject authority in the church?

- Worry is a huge problem in our secular societies. How would you explain why people worry? (Check out our book, Overcoming Anxiety: Finding Peace, Discovering God, for further information.)

LIVING HOPE IN A FALLEN WORLD
1 Peter

1 Peter 5:8-14 Study Questions

Final Advice for the Believers

Peter provides invaluable advice to those who struggle with difficult situations and harassing temptations during their short time on earth.

(1) The Need for Alertness (5:8-11)

Don't be caught off guard! A powerful diabolical being is planning an assault on your lives!

> ⁸Be of sober spirit, be on the alert. Your adversary, the devil, prowls about like a roaring lion, seeking someone to devour. ⁹But resist him, firm in your faith, knowing that the same experiences of suffering are being accomplished by your brethren who are in the world. ¹⁰And after you have suffered for a little while, the God of all grace, who called you to His eternal glory in Christ, will Himself perfect, confirm, strengthen and establish you. ¹¹To Him be dominion forever and ever. Amen" (1 Peter 5:8-11).

1. What are the two commands in the first part of verse 8?

2. How is a sober spirit different from a "drunken" one? What advantage does a sober spirit have (5:8)?

3. Who is the devil? What is his business (5:8)?

4. The devil roars as he seeks his prey. How does that help him in his pursuit? How does that spiritually work out when He is "catching" believers?

5. The devil is very powerful. What three ways believers can rightly respond to the devil (5:9)?

    ✦

    ✦

    ✦

6. Does the Lord promise that believers will never suffer (5:10)? Why do some believers think they will avoid this?

7. What does the Lord promise His people in verse 10?

8. Describe the meaning of "the God of all grace" (5:10)?

9. Notice the personal touch of the Lord during these trying times through the words "will Himself" (5:10). How might that help us in handling suffering?

10. Describe how each of these words differ from one another: perfect, confirm, strength, and establish (5:10). Use a dictionary as needed. Who does this? When will he do it?

11. Write down or say verse 11 aloud several times until you memorize it.

12. What does dominion imply?

13. Why do you think Peter ends with this praise (5:11)?

14. What is your greatest weakness? How does the evil one "get" you to fall?

15. What are the different spiritual disciplines and how do they help us maintain a vigilant Christian life?

Summary

Casual living ushers in trouble, whereas vigilance and purposed biblical thinking wards off the evil one.

(2) The Bond of Christ (5:12-14)

Peter ends this letter with carefully chosen words to the persecuted Christian believers, identifying his affinity between them and the danger he himself faced.

> ¹²Through Silvanus, our faithful brother (for so I regard him), I have written to you briefly, exhorting and testifying that this is the true grace of God. Stand firm in it! ¹³She who is in Babylon, chosen together with you, sends you greetings, and so does my son, Mark. ¹⁴Greet one another with a kiss of love. Peace be to you all who are in Christ (1 Peter 5:12-14).

16. What do we know about Silvanus here (5:12)?

17. What does it mean "through" Silvanus... I have written to you..."? (5:12). Also found in 2 Corinthians 1:19; 1 Thessalonians 1:1-2 Thessalonians 1:1?

18. What two words does Peter use to summarize the purpose of this letter (5:12)? Define each.

    ◆

    ◆

19. How is exhorting and testifying different? What does it mean that Peter testifies?

20. How would you summarize the meaning of the phrase, "the true grace of God" (5:12)?

21. "Stand firm in it" is figurative language. How could we otherwise convey this meaning?

22. Babylon lost its fame by Peter's time. Is Peter in the literal Babylon or is it a code word for Jerusalem or Rome where the persecution has broken out?

23. Why might Peter use a coded word?

24. What does the phrase "chosen together with you" mean (5:13)? (Also compare to 1 Peter 1:1, 2:9.)

25. Was Mark really Peter's son (5:13)? Explain.

26. How do God's people carry out this command today: "Greet one another with a kiss of love" (5:14)?

27. What kind of peace do you think Peter refers to in 5:14? (For further study, check out this resource).[5]

28. What simple wake-up call might you give yourself, your congregation or the church at large right now?

Summary

Though our lives might at times be comfortable, we need to be focus specifically on being like Christ rather than the world at large.

---

[5] https://www.foundationsforfreedom.net/Topics/AnxietyOA/OA01/OA01_13.html

Advanced Questions

- Where else does Peter use the word "sober" (5:8) in this book?

- What is the history of the devil (Ezra 14; Isaiah 28)?

- Why does God allow believers to suffer?

- Why does the devil seek to disturb believers' lives?

General questions on the Book of 1 Peter

- Pick out two main themes from 1 Peter and trace their development throughout the book.

- What was one verse or teaching from 1 Peter that has most significantly helped you? Memorize and explain.

Appendix #1: About the Author

Paul J. Bucknell is the president and founder of *Biblical Foundations for Freedom (BFF)*. Through his many books and extensive library of articles on the Bible, Paul makes known the power of the scriptures to build up and strengthen God's people so that they need not be ashamed. Paul's passion is to revive the people of God and see them living Christ-filled lives. He regularly trains Christian international leaders around the world. Paul and his wife, Linda, have eight children and five grandchildren. They presently live in Pittsburgh, Pennsylvania, USA.

www.ingramcontent.com/pod-product-compliance
Lightning Source LLC
Chambersburg PA
CBHW071310060426
42444CB00034B/1763